52 things to keep your husband
out of your hair when he retires.

The world's best-selling
retirement guide by R. J. Leggott.

For Mum and Dad.

And Chris, who is everything to me.

Old age can take our bodies and our looks, but it
can never take away how much we love each other.

First published in 2007.

USA edition.

Special thanks to Murray & Jo Nicholls, Lisa Upton,
Greg & Joe Bearup, Paul Jeffress, Calli Brown, Cal
Paterson, Zali and Chris Kirby.

ISBN 978 0 6151 7359 7

52 things to keep your husband out of your hair when he retires.

This is a survival manual. It will prepare you for the greatest challenge you've ever faced - your huband's retirement.

Soon he's going to be at home all the time; 24 hours a day, 7 days a week. He'll be right behind you wherever you go, sticking his nose into things that you've quite capably managed for the last 40 years or more. There's no question you love him, but compared to retirement, menopause will seem like a walk in the park.

The trick is to keep him busy, make him useful, and perhaps most importantly, make it all seem like it was his idea!

One for every week of the year.

There are 52 projects in this book. One for every week of the year. If he seems to be losing interest in one project, quickly switch him to another. By the end of his first year, he'll have found four or five projects that will perpetually keep him out of your hair and let you get on with what you love.

No. 01

Release some hot air.

If your husband has always got something to say, a blog is the perfect soapbox for him. It'll give him an outlet and protect your eardrums. A blog is an online diary that anyone can read. Post photos, rants, poetry, ideas, inventions – anything that takes his fancy or sets him off. It's as simple as going online and letting loose!

> Start here:
www.blogger.com

No. 02

Tell people where to go.

If he's never wrong and always knows the best route to take, there's a place for people like him – the local gallery, stadium or 'place of interest'. The tourist industry is always looking for volunteers to help out, telling people where to go, how to get there and how the place came to be. It'll take him off your hands and he may learn something he didn't know. Not that he'd admit it.

> **Start here:**
your local tourist information centre

THIS WAY

No. 03

Turn water into gold.

American men are drinking less beer than ever, but they are drinking more boutique beers. Quantity down, quality up. Surprise him with a Home Brew Starter kit and get him out of the house and into the garage creating his own special brew. Quality ingredients will make your place the toast of the neighborhood.

> Start here:
www.brewingusa.com

No. 04

Turn the grandkids into superheroes.

Kids love being told a story. Now imagine if they were the hero. It's magical when a story includes their friends, pets and places they see and experience every day. Add in your own digital pictures and you've got a family best seller. Putting it all together will keep him busy and the grandkids will never tire of it being read to them.

> Start here:
pen, paper and a touch of imagination

No. 05

Repulse the monkey.

He may not move like a gazelle now, but after a few weeks of Tai Chi he'll start to limber up, improve his health, concentration and overall well-being. And with moves like *Golden Cock Stands on One Leg, Carry Tiger and Return to Mountain* and *Part Wild Horses Mane,* he'll have a tale to share with his buddies, too.

> Start here:
www.usataichi.org or
check your local newspaper for classes

猴

No. 06

Put a panther in his pocket.

There's a reason your husband's ears have been getting hairier as he gets older – they're a perfect sanctuary for wildlife. The National Wildlife Refuge Association is a network of hundreds of volunteers who work to protect this country's diverse wildlife. And you don't have to live in the wilderness to help out, there are critters in need of TLC across the country.

> **Start here:**
www.fws.gov or www.refugenet.org

No. 07

Solve the chicken and egg once and for all.

Just because he's retired doesn't mean he has to mothball his mind. Big companies like Procter & Gamble, Boeing and DuPont are outsourcing their Research and Development to the public, offering anyone the chance to try and solve problems they can't crack. One thing is certain - spending the pocket money he earns won't be a problem.

> Start here:
www.innocentive.com or
Mechanical Turk at www.amazon.com

No. 08

Ride the swell.

Every red-blooded American male owes it to The Beach Boys to give surfing a go before he pops his clogs. You get to catch the sun, while he tries to catch a wave. Forget the old wives' tale about old dogs and new tricks, he'll get hooked on his first tube.

> Start here:
www.surfschools.com

No.
09

Make a
royal flush.

You're never going to get your spring chicken out
of the house with lawn bowls or bridge. Instead,
lure him with the thrill of Texas Hold 'Em.
It's easy to learn, the gambling is only for kudos
and he'll meet a bunch of friends that will
regularly take him out of your hair. Everyone's
a winner. Community events are popping up
across the country.

> Start here:
your neighborhood club or newspaper

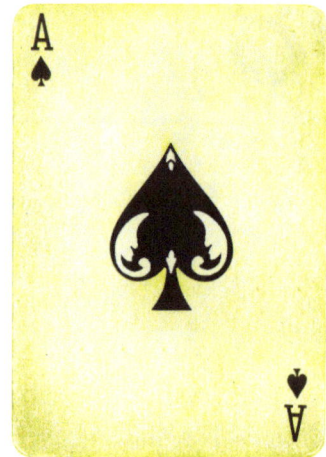

No. 10

Put the old vegetable to good use.

It's not his taste buds that have gone, it's the taste of vegetables. Heirloom vegetables have a rich flavor you won't find in the supermarket. Heirloom vegetables are open pollinated, so your man will not only be kept busy growing and tending the vegetables, but he'll have to save and store the seeds for next year.

> Start here:
www.seedsavers.org

No. 11

Show him the door.

Walking is good for his heart and great for your head. Send him for the morning newspaper. Send him for bread. Ask him to pop out and check on old Mr McQuilty around the corner. Pack several tasks into one journey, and he'll develop a longer route and be less likely to take the car. Send him at the same time every day to turn a 'one-off' trip into a habit.

> Start here:
your front door with a pair of sneakers

No. 12

**Put more lead
in his pencil.**

There's no man who doesn't want to be the best lover in the world. Why shouldn't it be your husband? Better sex makes you both happy. In the Kama Sutra, there are positions to suit every level of inertia and girth. He already reads in the bathroom, just replace the sports pages with the Kama Sutra.

> Start here:
A Lover's Guide to the Kama Sutra,
Virginia Reynolds.

No. 13

Roll in
the dough.

Turn the old breadwinner into the bread maker.
The process of kneading, rising and baking will
enthrall him for hours – with delicious results.
Forget the machines, if he's not going to do it
right he may as well buy it from the supermarket. For best results, use fresh yeast, not dried.

> Start here:
The Essential Baking Cookbook,
Murdoch Books, 2000.

No. 14

Find a new audience.

If you've heard all your husband's stories before, it's time to inflict them on someone else. Meals on Wheels lets people live independent lives in their own home and provides vital contact with the outside world, as well as offering nutritious meals. It's also a great way to discover America's diversity in culture, religion, language and more. Better still, he doesn't have to cook a thing.

> **Start here:**
Meals on Wheels, www.mowaa.org

No. 15

Rediscover the basement floor.

People are making fortunes online from the junk in their attics. All you need is a digital camera, a computer and an Internet connection. Soon you could have your garage clear and enough dough for your next vacation. The more of a hoarder your husband is, the longer he'll be entertained, and the more cash you're likely to make.

> Start here:
www.ebay.com

No. 16

Say goodbye
to the in-laws.

Tracing his family history may seem like a job for old folk, but there are extraordinary finds to be had. Especially if he discovers:

    a) he was adopted and your wicked in-laws are impostors, or

    b) he's the only heir to a small fortune from a now defunct pork-belly empire.

Of course, seeing his cheeky grin echo back generations can be reward enough.

> Start here:
The National Archives, www.archives.gov

Count to nine.

Here's something that will keep him quiet for hours and all he needs to do is count to nine. Sudoku is a simple logical puzzle that has taken the world by storm. All he needs to do is fill a 9x9 grid so that every column, every row and every 3x3 box contains the digits 1 to 9. Sound like child's play? It's more addictive than peanuts at a pachyderm convention.

> Start here:
your daily newspaper or www.sudoku.com

No. 18

Keep an eye on the world.

Shift his focus from the state of his ingrown toenail to the planet's health with a few weather-measuring instruments. Start simple with a thermometer, rain gauge, wind vane, barometer and a book on clouds and he can start recording the heavens. Soon he'll be able to track and predict the weather. After all, he can't do any worse than the people on the 6 o'clock news.

> **> Start here:**
American Meteorological Society,
www.ametsoc.org

No. 19

Push aside Spielberg.

To make it big in the movies, you don't need a Hollywood studio or an expensive camera. These days a cell phone can do the trick. They have quality video cameras and also come with software to edit footage on your computer. He doesn't have to win an Oscar with his first attempt, but a trip to Cannes would be nice.

> Start here:
a cell phone with built-in video camera

No. 20

Shake up Wall Street.

For as little as $500 he can play with the big men who stride the world's trading floors. Online stock trading sites put the stock markets within reach of anyone and include research tools, charts and recommendations from industry experts. As he grows his portfolio, he can use dividends to fund his next trade (or your next girl's night out).

> Start here:
www.etrade.com

No. 21

Put the words into someone else's mouth.

Getting by in this world is hard enough without all the newspapers, road signs and jelly labels being a jumble of gobbledygook. People who can't read aren't stupid, just illiterate. Helping someone to read will stop him grumbling about his eyesight – and will transform someone's life.

> Start here:
National Institute for Literacy,
www.nifl.com

No.
22

Beat the grandkids.

Computer games aren't just about shooting zombies and spilling as much blood as possible. PlayStation® and Xbox® have games of skill that are designed to challenge his mind, stave off the loony bin and get the feeling back into his hands. Visits to grandpa's won't be such a chore for the grandkids, either.

> Start here:
your local electrical retailer

No. 23

Pursue immortality.

By the time he's got to his age, he's learnt to do more than just change the TV remote. He's not going to live forever, but his talents can. Skills, customs and languages are fast disappearing, simply because no one is learning them – and no one is offering to teach them. Identify his talents, write them down and offer free lessons.

> Start here:
your local notice board & newspaper

No. 24

Turn the sidewalk into a grocery store.

Few things get him as excited as the words: All you can eat. Now he can create his own smorgasbord on your street. Permaculture does away with mass agriculture and nurtures a smaller, intimately woven fabric of plants that become a permanent, sustainable supply of food.

> Start here:
www.permacultureinternational.org
or visit your local bookstore

No. 25

Shake his hips before they break.

You both used to shake your booty, now you're lucky if you stand up to do the Chicken Dance at weddings. Music will wind his clock back and give him new pep in his pickle. Incredible musicians are performing every night of the week; jazz, rock, new folk, doof, indie, ska, hip hop: give it all a chance.

> Start here:
music listings in newspapers or
www.timeout.com

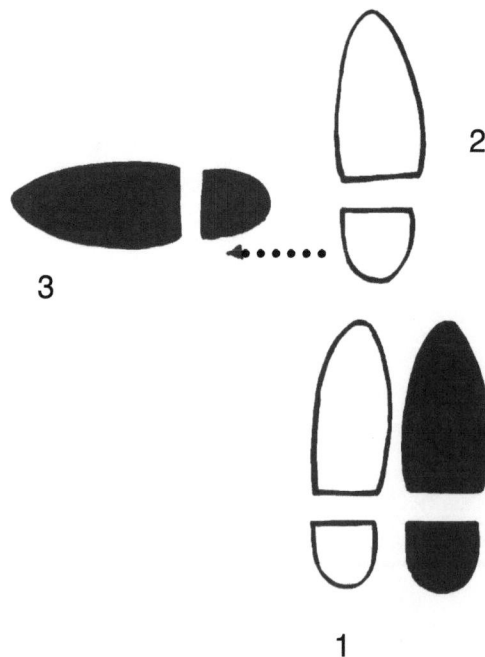

2

3

1

No. 26

Do the wild thing under the stars.

Stir up his desire with trips to the wilderness. Hiking and camping doesn't have to be painful and uncomfortable anymore. Quality tents, boots and sleeping gear can create the Hilton in the hinterlands. Start easy by driving to remote campsites and taking short hikes. Rediscover the great American outdoors and your unbridled passion.

> Start here:
National Park Service, www.nps.gov

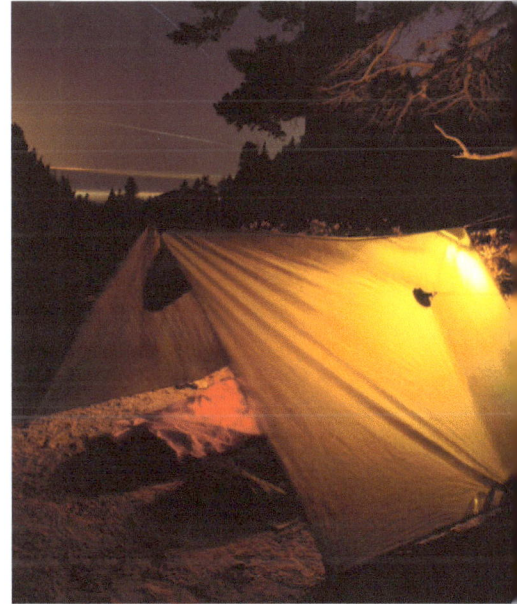

No. 27

Speak in tongues.

Every two weeks someone takes a language to the grave. Dying languages rob the world of a unique culture and way of life. It's not enough to simply learn the language, you need to pass it on. Choose a language that fascinates and dive in - from Scottish Gaelic to Amazonian Iquitos to Aboriginal and Native American languages.

> Start here:
The Green Book of Language Revitalization,
Academic Press, 2001.

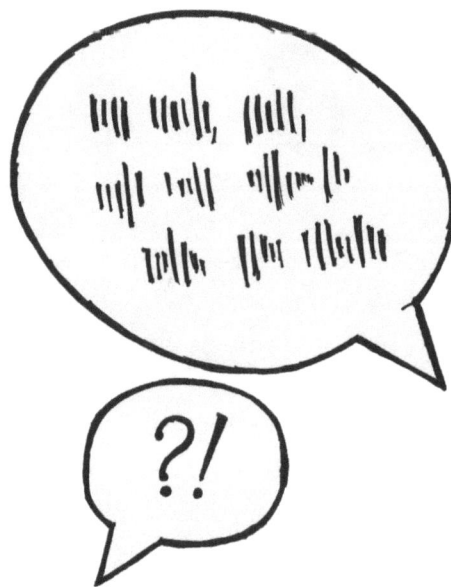

No. 28

Plunder the airwaves.

Podcasts are like radio programs 'broadcast' over the Internet. Anyone can create a podcast – it's simply an audio recording put on the net. Singing, talking, interviews, music shows or even the sound of birds in your neighborhood. People go online, download them and listen to them on their computer or MP3 player (iPod). Stop him talking to himself, get him talking to the world.

> Start here:
www.podcastalley.com

No. 29

Invite yourself to dinner.

If you've run out of conversation over dinner, there's a better solution than switching on the television. Just invite yourself to a neighbor's house. Progressive dinners let you dine, talk and walk. One course at every house. Put him in charge of the progressive dinner committee, let him plan the route, menu and wine.

> Start here:
a good cookbook and hungry neighbours

No. 30

**Find a
long lost friend.**

Sometimes in life your man loses his friends.
Friends he should have held on to. It's not
because he is particularly clumsy, but they've
simply dropped off the radar when you've
moved house or changed jobs. Now he can find
them again and start where he left off.

> Start here:
www.facebook.com or www.palseeker.com

RETURNED
TO
SENDER

No Such Street
Directory Clerk

No. 31

Start another family.

You did your part by humping throughout the 1960s and 1970s and now your brood has spread to generations of children, grand-children and (heaven forbid) great-grandchildren. Why stop now? Sponsoring a child in the States or abroad will keep him busy with letters, photos and changing the world.

> Start here:
www.worldvision.org
www.care.org

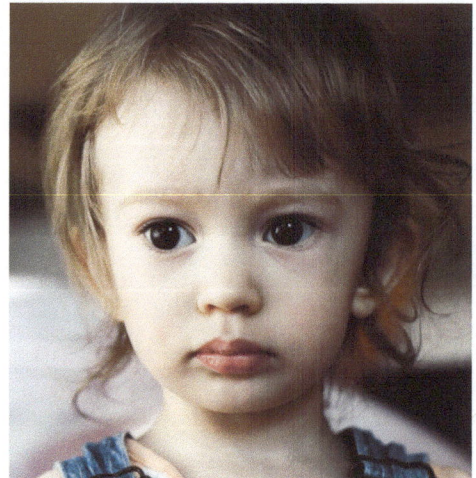

No. 32

Perk up.

He may have not made the cut for law school, but there's no reason he can't be a barista. Unless you're a Mormon, coffee is the most socially acceptable drug in the world. Forget instant coffee, it's all about organic fair trade beans, unscorched coffee and frothy milk. Little wonder there are courses to get it right. Enroll him and you'll wake up to the best coffee on your street.

> Don't start here:
Starbucks

No. 33

Challenge the sword with a pen.

Part of the reason your relationship has lasted so long is that you can tell each other exactly what you think. For many people, speaking their mind has landed them in jail, facing torture and untold horrors. Yet it's frighteningly simple to defend human rights. One letter turns into a tsunami of protest and the authorities are forced to yield. Donate time, money or both.

> Start here:
www.amnesty.org

No.
34

Watch the birdie.

The old man may have a few surprises in him yet. Photography is an easily accessible art form and lets you see the world through someone else's eyes. Set him up with a digital camera and send him packing, shooting the streets, its people and places through his eyes. Catch fleeting moments forever and see his true heart. As Cartier-Bresson said, "This is the poetry of life's reality."

> Start here:
buy a digital camera and color printer

No. 35

Shout at the kids, not the TV.

Put his sporting passion to good use. If he missed out on the State team because of an unfortunate knee injury, he can relive his dreams through tomorrow's talent. Every weekend thousands of kids take to fields across the country. If someone can turn them into winners, it's your husband. And if his team doesn't take the cup, simply switch codes or even sports. Anyone for hurling?

> Start here:
volunteer coaches or referees at your local sporting club

No. 36

Solve a mystery.

Put the skills of deduction your husband learned in Clue® to good use. Find an unsolved case and get him in the library rechecking case histories. Or engage him on a stake out with those suspicious neighbors down the street. It doesn't matter if he finds anything or not, it will keep him out of the house for hours.

> Start here:
www.crimestopusa.com

No. 37

Don't throw them back.

Your man can now use fishing as an excuse to protect the environment. By fishing for introduced fish and only throwing back native species he can help eradicate noxious species. By joining fish restocking programs, he can double his conservation efforts. You couldn't have found a better or more useful way to get him out of the house.

> Start here:
your local angling club

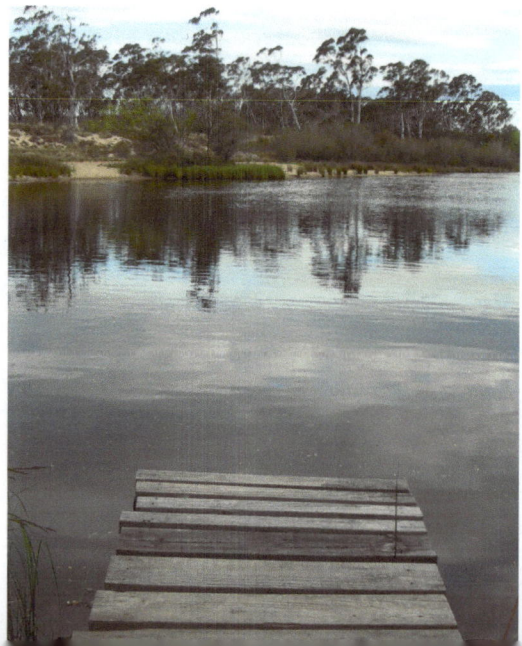

No. 38

Don a beret.

Discover the poet inside your man. After years of marriage, it's easy to forget how romantically it all began. It's time to rekindle the spark in him. Poetry doesn't have to be all roses and cherubs, but an open mind and the confidence to share his inner voice can reveal a stranger who'll turn you on.

> Start here:
www.poems.com

No. 39

Go fly a kite.

If your only conversation about wind centers on his flatulence, it's time to get him to the park. Kite flying, fights and stunts are no longer the realm of kids. It's a dog eat dog eat world where fine glass is woven into string and killer instincts come to the fore. It'll build his fitness and keep him in the basement crafting the perfect fighting machine.

> Start here:
American Kitefliers Association, www.aka.kite.org

No. 40

Discover a
red-blooded American.

Red wine is good for his heart, but he doesn't have to take it medicinally. Even the most ardent beer drinker can learn a thing or two about what makes a good tipple. It'll make dining out an experience and impress the pants off your fancy relatives. Next thing, he'll be under the house digging out a wine cellar.

> Start here:
Wine tastings at your local liquor store.

No. 41

Stop the rot.

Luckily for you, you've got each other to tell you if you're dead. For a lot of people, there's no one to hold a mirror to their mouth. Sign him up as a volunteer to the American Red Cross and every morning he can call an elderly person in their home to check on them. It's a daily morale boost, relieving their isolation and helping them maintain their independence.

> Start here:
The American Red Cross; www.redcross.org

No. 42

Talk to an alien.

While sometimes he might think you're from another planet, that's nothing compared to what other people think is out there. Get him to set the record straight. Start by downloading the PlanetQuest screensaver, which searches the galaxy for extra terrestrial life, then progress to telescopes, infrared alien detectors and more. He might not find life out there, but it'll give him a new lease on life.

> Start here:
Search for Extra Terrestrial Intelligence;
www.seti.org

No. 43

Explore the far reaches of his palate.

Make dining out an exploration. Every week your man has to find a new place to eat. Start off easy at the local Italian restaurant or club, then let him take it from there. Let him research, let him make reservations and let him find the old romantic inside him.

> Start here:
www.zagat.com

No. 44

Hit a natural high.

You've got plenty of time to fill your bellies with pills and start rattling around. Get him outside and establish a natural therapy garden. He'll keep busy looking after it and learning the plant's medicinal values, you'll have an abundance of fresh herbs for the kitchen. If you catch him smoking his herbs, you'll know he's planted the wrong type.

> Start here:
Encyclopedia of herbal medicine,
Andrew Chevallier, 2000.

No. 45

Banish empty walls forever.

You've probably spent the best part of your married life trying to get a paintbrush in his hand to take care of the peeling walls and front fence. Here's a way to make sure he's always keen to get out the coveralls. Put a blank canvas in front of him and coax out the inner Picasso.

> Start here:
your local arts store or
community education college

No. 46

Get a sheriff's badge.

He won't be able to jail people or stick them up with his six-shooter, but as a Notary Public your partner can still wield authority. He can act as a critical witness for documents and oversee the swearing of oaths. It might not be the deputy sheriff post he dreamed of as a kid, but it'll impress the grandkids.

> **Start here:**
www.nationalnotary.org

No. 47

Commune
with the dead.

It seems ghosts aren't too handy with secateurs and neither are some graveyard caretakers. The gorgeous architecture and timeless stories of our cemeteries are overgrown and neglected. The only people paying attention to them are vandals. It's time to take care of the dead - and it's nice to think someone will do it for you one day.

> Start here:
your local cemetery

No. 48

Give him kicks at night and on the weekends.

Season passes to sport, opera or theater are a sure ticket to maintaining your sanity. You can look forward to him heading out on weekends to the footy or at night to see a play or concert. You'll get much needed head space and guilt-free time to hang out with the girls.

> Start here:
your team's club, the local theater or concert hall

No. 49

Habla Espanol?

Your husband might not always listen to you, but he's certain to take a tip from the Statue of Liberty. She has always welcomed hard-working men and women who want to make America their home. And now your man can help out, too. Teaching English, encouraging American traditions and more.

> Start here:
www.usafreedomcorps.gov

No.
50

Plan your escape.

For years you've been telling him where to go. This is his chance to return the favour. There are over 200 countries in the world to explore, not to mention the endless places in the States to discover. Set him a budget and let him go wild, planning the flights, the sights, the drives, the routes, the accommodation, the works. You don't need big budgets, just big imaginations.

> Start here:
The Times Atlas of the World.

No. 51

Strike a chord.

Sometimes he might make you feel like beating
your head against the wall – yet the antidote may
be introducing him to a beat. From his singing
in the shower, it may be hard to believe there's
a musician in him, but a good tutor can work
miracles. Let him choose an instrument, find
him a patient tutor, and he'll get lost for hours
in his inner symphonies.

> Start here:
your local choir, community college or noticeboard

No. 52

Send him
back to work.

If all else fails, pack his lunch and send him back to work. There are plenty of companies looking for experienced people who can work part-time on flexible hours. In fact, consulting can reap big rewards and enormous kudos - it also lets him share his big ideas with someone else other than you. Part-time work means you see each other when you want to, rather than when you have to.

> Start here:
www.monster.com

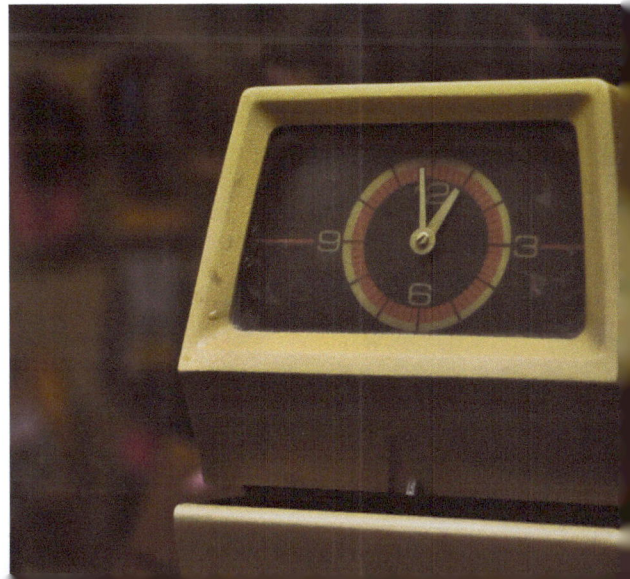

www.ingramcontent.com/pod-product-compliance
Lightning Source LLC
Chambersburg PA
CBHW060802270326
41926CB00002B/70